GIRLS ROCK!

Camping Chaos

Shey Kettle

illustrated by
Meredith Thomas

First Published in Great Britain by
RISING STARS UK LTD 2006
22 Grafton Street, London, W1S 4EX

For more information visit our website at:
www.risingstars-uk.com

British Library Cataloguing in Publication Data
A CIP record for this book is available from the British Library.

ISBN: 978-1-84680-068-9

First published in 2006 by
MACMILLAN EDUCATION AUSTRALIA PTY LTD
627 Chapel Street, South Yarra 3141

Visit our website at www.macmillan.com.au or go directly to
www.macmillanlibrary.com.au

Associated companies and representatives throughout the world.

Series created by Felice Arena and Phil Kettle
Project management by Limelight Press Pty Ltd
Cover and text design by Lore Foye
Illustrations by Meredith Thomas
Printed in China

UK Editorial by Westcote Computing Editorial Services

GIRLS ROCK!
CONTENTS

Mai   *Carly*

CHAPTER 1

We're Away!

Carly and Mai are going camping in
the summer holidays with Carly's
Mum.

Mai "I'm so pleased that your Mum's
asked me to come. It'll be so cool."

Carly "I can't believe Mum thinks four bags are too many to take camping."

Mai "I don't think mothers realise that great adventurers like us get really dirty and need to change our clothes all the time."

Carly "Yes, but mine will when she has to wash our clothes."

Mai "Do you think there'll be other kids at the camp site?"

Carly "I hope so. Last year I met these really cool girls, Jess and Rachel, and we did everything together."

Mai "Maybe they'll be there again."

Carly "I hope so. You'd really like them."

Mai "I'm really glad we're sharing
a tent. Last time I went camping I
had to sleep in the same tent as my
stinky brother."

Carly "Ugh, gross!"

Mai "Boys always smell really bad ...
especially brothers."

Carly "And they snore, too."

4

CHAPTER 2

Tent Spotting

They head off and arrive at the camp site two hours later.

Mai "This place is brilliant."
Carly "You're right. Let's set up our tent near the water."

Mai "Cool! Then we can sit right
outside and fish."

Carly "And I'll catch the biggest fish
ever with my new rod."

Mai "You mean the second biggest
fish. My rod may be old, but it's
been around. It knows the best and
biggest fish to catch."

Carly "I wish we didn't bring all these bags, there's hardly any room now for our sleeping bags."

Mai "I know. It didn't look that much when we were packing."

Carly "Oh well, if we have to sleep with it all, at least clothes are soft."

Mai "Well, just don't tell your Mum that we brought too much. She'll tell my Mum and then they'll think that they're right ... again."

Carly "Why do they always just know things?"

The girls both sigh.

CHAPTER 3

A Juicy Idea

After pitching their tent, Carly and Mai have a rest on the beach.

Mai "What shall we do first, fishing or exploring?"

Carly "Both. We can go exploring to find a great place to fish!"

Mai "Excellent!"

Carly "We could paddle ourselves
out to sea on our surf boards and
look for a whole new place where
nobody's ever been ... while we fish!"

Mai "Great idea. But what if we
catch a huge fish on the end of our
line?"

Carly "We might get towed to the other side of the world and never be heard of again."

Mai "As if, but maybe it's not such a good idea to paddle out. We wouldn't want to get stranded. Let's get going. I'll get the bait."

Mai gets a bucket of worms out of the back of the car.

Mai "Look, there are loads of big, juicy worms."

Carly "Good, fish love worms."

Mai "I wonder why?"

Carly "They must taste good."

Mai "Yes, so why don't we eat them … cooked on the barbeque with heaps of tomato sauce?"

Carly (holding a worm) "If you think they're so good, why don't you try one then?"

Mai "No thanks! Worms are gross enough without eating them, too!"

Carly "I think the worst thing about fishing is cleaning the fish. If I catch any, I'm going to let them go."

Mai "Me, too. The only fish I want to eat are from the fish and chip shop."

CHAPTER 4

Island Girls

The girls spot a sand bank about forty metres from the shore.

Mai "Look at that sand sticking up above the water. It's like an island."

Carly "Let's wade out there and fish."

The girls collect all they need for their great adventure—fishing rods, a bucket and the worms. They put on their life jackets and some sun block.

Mai "Why are you putting your trainers on when we're about to walk through water?"

Carly "Haven't you ever heard of crabs? Well, they've got great big claws … and we have toes!"

Mai "Right, I get the picture. I think I'll wear my trainers, too. I want to make sure I keep all my toes!"

Mai and Carly wade through the
water towards the sand bank.

Mai "I really do feel like a great
explorer."
Carly "So do I. It's like we've just
discovered a whole new country.
I think the fish near this island will
be huge."

Mai "Yes, they'll be gigantic because nobody's ever tried to catch them."

The girls step on to the sand.

Carly "I claim this island in the name of Carly and Mai."

Mai "May it be our place forever ... or at least for the holidays!"

Carly "So, what'll we call our island?"

Mai "It needs a really cool name."

Carly "How about Girls Island?"

Mai "Yes, that's a great name. Let's write it in the sand."

The girls write "Girls Island" in large letters in the sand.

Mai "Now, anybody that comes near it will know it's ours."

Carly "I know what else we could write in the sand."

Carly writes "No boys allowed".

Mai "I hope that keeps them away. We don't want our island polluted."

Carly "With boy germs! Yuk! Come on, it's time we caught some really big fish."

The girls take off their life jackets. Carly pulls a big worm from the bucket and shows it to Mai.

Carly "This'll catch a really big fish."

Carly threads the worm onto the
hook.

Mai "Doesn't that hurt the worm?"
Carly "I don't think so. It's probably
  just like getting your ear pierced."
Mai "But without the ice! Hey, I think
  our island is starting to shrink."

Carly "What? Perhaps the tide's come in but it shouldn't come in any further. Trust me."

Mai (worriedly) "OK Miss Expert. I hope you're right. That water's pretty close to us now."

The girls cast out their lines. Soon Carly gets a bite.

Carly (gripping her rod hard) "I think
I've caught the biggest fish in the
whole sea."

Mai "It must be a whale."

Carly "Whales aren't fish, they're
mammals. Help me, Mai, my arms
are about to be pulled off."

Mai grabs onto Carly's fishing rod
and helps her to reel in the fish.

Mai "Perhaps it's one of those fish
with the razor-sharp teeth."

Carly "Yes well, whatever it is,
it's huge."

Mai "Keep reeling it in, Carly. I'm
sure it's getting closer."

CHAPTER 5

Trouble in Paradise

Soon there is a huge fish flapping about on the sand.

Mai "What do we do with it now we've caught it?"

Carly "I think we should let it go."

Mai "So do I, but it's going to be hard to move and we have to get rid of the hook."

Carly "Can you grab its tail?"

Carly and Mai manage to drag the fish back into the water. As they do, the hook drops out of its mouth and the fish swims away.

Mai "Off you go fishy, back where you belong."

Carly "That was fun, but exhausting! Let's have a rest."

Carly and Mai lie down on the sand and look up at the sky.

Mai "That cloud looks like a car."

Carly "And that one looks like a great fisherman ... just like me!"

As the girls stare into the sky, they feel their toes getting wet. Suddenly, they spring to their feet. They can't believe their eyes.

Carly "Oh no! The tide's come in and our island's nearly covered."
Mai "What now, Miss Expert?"

The girls put their life jackets back on and gather their belongings. They wade into the water.

Carly "It's too deep. We could swim but we'll never get all our things back. We need someone to help."

Mai "But no one's around and your Mum's gone to make lunch."

Carly "We'll just have to yell. Heeellppp! Soommeonnee!"

Just then, the girls spot a man in a dinghy some distance away.

Mai (waving her arms) "Hey mister, heeelpp! We can't get back."
Carly and Mai (shouting) "Heeelp!"

The man looks up and sees the girls. He motors over and picks them up.

Mai "Thanks mister. That was close! We nearly lost all our things."

Carly "The camp site really looks
good and I'm starving. I don't think
Mum will be too pleased about this
though. She's always telling me to
keep an eye on the tides."

Mai "Yes, but we can say we
discovered a brand new island."

Carly (pointing) "Yes right, and that
we lost one, too!"

Mai

GIRLS ROCK!
Camping Lingo

Carly

air bed A bed filled with air that you sleep on in a tent.

ear plugs Small plugs you put in your ears to block out noise. A must for camping in case you sleep next to someone who snores.

guy rope What each tent peg is tied to. Lots of these ropes are attached to the tent to keep it steady.

space blanket A really thin sheet of foil-covered material that rolls up to nothing but is really warm. Astronauts first used them in space!

tent peg A stick that the guy rope attaches to. You stick it in the ground.

Camping Must-dos

☆ Make sure you don't pitch your tent *too* close to the water's edge. The tide might come in and fill your tent.

☆ Always wear a hat when you are outside during the day. The sun can be fierce!

☆ If you sleepwalk, tie a guy rope to your leg then around a tent peg so you don't go wandering around in the middle of the night.

☆ Always take a torch to bed with you. There is nothing worse than going to the toilet and not being able to find your way through all those creepy-crawlies outside—eek!

☆ Take plenty of food, especially yummy stuff like marshmallows to toast over a campfire.

☆ Take plenty of clothes. There will always be a reason to change your clothes at least three times a day!

☆ Make sure that you put out the campfire before you go to bed.

☆ Bring enough bait so that you can catch plenty of fish.

☆ Always tell an adult if you are going away from the camp site in case you get lost or stranded on an island!

GIRLS ROCK!

Camping
Instant Info

Tents can be very simple or very fancy. The most basic tent is a temporary shelter made from fabric draped between two poles.

Tents have been used since the Stone Age. They have protected people from weather, and have provided space for gatherings.

The highest tides on Earth occur in Nova Scotia's Minas Basin in Canada.

Tents come in lots of different sizes. The most popular is the two-person tent.

Girl Guides spend a lot of time camping. The first Girl Guides were led by Agnes Baden-Powell (the sister of the man who founded the Boy Scouts) in 1918.

The best tents have mosquito nets and fly screens, which stop you from getting bitten by all the creepy-crawlies out there.

There are camp sites all over the world. Camping is one of the most popular types of holiday for families.

Think Tank

1   How many people can sleep in a
    two-person tent?

2   What is a space blanket?

3   Where does a space blanket get its
    name from?

4   What country has the highest tides in
    the world?

5   Does a guy rope have anything to
    do with Guy Fawkes?

6   How do you keep creepy-crawlies
    out of your tent?

7   What is one of the yummiest foods
    to cook over a campfire?

8   How do you deal with snorers in a
    tent?

Answers

8 You deal with snorers in a tent by wearing ear plugs.

7 Marshmallows are yummy to cook over a campfire.

6 Use a mosquito net or fly screen to keep creepy-crawlies out of your tent.

5 No, a guy rope keeps your tent steady.

4 Canada has the highest tides in the world.

3 Space blankets were first used by astronauts in space, which is where they get their name from.

2 A space blanket is a thin sheet of foil-covered material that keeps you warm.

1 Two people sleep in a two-person tent, of course!

How did you score?

- If you got all 8 answers correct, you're ready to go camping in the big, wide world.

- If you got 6 answers correct, then perhaps you should sleep in the same tent as your parents for a while.

- If you got fewer than 4 answers correct, stick to hotels when you go away.

Hey Girls!

I hope that you have as much fun reading my story as I have had writing it. I loved reading and writing stories when I was young.

At school, why don't you use "Camping Chaos" as a play and you and your friends can be the actors.

Bring in some fishing equipment from home. Use sheets for the tents. Maybe you could have your play outside and make a campfire.

So ... have you decided who is going to be Mai and who is going to be Carly? Now, with your friends, read and act out this play in front of your classmates. It'll definitely make the whole class laugh.

You can also take the story home and get someone to act out the parts with you.

So, get ready to have more fun with your reading than the Easter Bunny at Easter!

And remember, Girls Rock!

Shey Kettle.

GIRLS ROCK!
When We Were Kids

Shey · Jacqueline

Shey talked to Jacqueline, another *Girls Rock!* author.

Shey "Did you go camping when you were little?"

Jacqueline "Yes! We camped by the river but I didn't like it."

Shey "Why not?"

Jacqueline "Well, when I went to sleep, the world's biggest mosquitoes bit me."

Shey "Really, how big were they?"

Jacqueline "They were so big that they carried me 100 metres from my tent."

Shey "Oh no! How did you get back?"

Jacqueline "I woke up!"

GIRLS ROCK!
What a Laugh!

Q Why didn't the skeleton go camping?

A He had no body to go with!

GIRLS ROCK!

The Sleepover

Pool Pals

Bowling Buddies

Girl Pirates

Netball Showdown

School Play Stars

Diary Disaster

Horsing Around

Newspaper Scoop

Snowball Attack

Dog on the Loose

Escalator Escapade

Cooking Catastrophe

Talent Quest

Wild Ride

Camping Chaos

Mummy Mania

Skater Chicks

GIRLS ROCK! books are available from most booksellers. For mail order information please call Rising Stars on 0870 40 20 40 8 or visit www.risingstars-uk.com